Contents

Barney and the Magic Mirror
Learning activities:

Acknowledgments

The Police Community Clubs of Great Britain would like to thank the following for their contribution to this publication:
Published by Ian Jackson
Edited By Kelly Griffiths, Dave Forster & Richard Evans
Norman Kirtlan for creative ideas
Paul Hogg and Chris Fairley for graphic design
Julie Poad for learning activities
Community Initiatives Associates for sales and distribution

The Barney and Echo Series

The Barney and Echo series has been developed to support parents and teachers in addressing personal, social and health education (PSHE) at key stage 1-2. The books are set in Treetop Forest and follow the adventures of Barney Eagle and Echo Squirrel.

Each title has a story relating to a PSHE subject area with activities to reinforce the learning goals. The books, which are designed to be fun and educational, can be used in a classroom setting and at home to support reading and discussion.

The series of five books also contains titles that address issues such as anti-social behaviour, internet safety and bullying. In total, the books have been distributed to more than 350,000 children across the UK.

In this title, Barney and Echo have to help their friends, Spike Hedgehog, Dizzy Rabbit and Digsby Mole when they get involved with drugs, tobacco and alcohol. At first, Barney doesn't know what to do to help, but then Tom Stoat the Woodland Wizard shows him a magic mirror that he can use to see into the future.

Barney and the Magic Mirror looks at what the future could hold for Spike, Dizzy and Digsby if they don't change their behaviour and then shows how much better they feel when they do. The story is supplemented by activities to help children understand what drugs, alcohol and tobacco can do to their bodies and to help them make good decisions.

Barney and the Magic Mirror

One day, Barney Eagle
was visiting his friend
Echo Squirrel in hospital.
Echo had been playing in
the forest and had fallen
on to a piece of sharp
glass. The glass came from
a broken bottle which
someone had carelessly
thrown away.

Poor Echo had a big cut
on his foot and now had
a huge white bandage
wrapped around it.

Barney was sad to think that
some people didn't care
about where they left
broken bottles and litter.

Treetop Forest was his home and he cared about it very much.

"I'll go back later and pick it up," he said to Echo. "I don't want anyone
else to hurt themselves."

Earlier that day Barney had been to see his old friend Tom Stoat the Woodland Wizard.

Tom had given Barney a special present, it was a Magic Mirror.

Echo's foot was very painful and Barney could see that he needed cheering up, so he showed his friend the Magic Mirror that Tom Stoat the Woodland Wizard had given to him. "Take a look, Echo," said Barney. "Tell me what you see."

Echo sat up and took hold of the mirror.

"It's just a mirror," he said, smiling at his friend, but when Echo saw his reflection, he got quite a shock.

"I….I can see me," Echo stammered. "But my leg is better and I'm running around the forest playing football."

4

Barney laughed. "It's a magic mirror, Echo. A mirror that can see into the future."

Now that Barney had cheered Echo up, he set off to find the broken glass. It wasn't long before he reached the clearing by the old mill. When he got there, he didn't just see one bottle, he saw lots and lots. The ground was covered with bottles, drinks cans, cigarette packets and even a needle lying in the short grass.

Barney couldn't believe what he was looking at.

"Oh dear," he squawked.

"What am I going to do now?"

As he was thinking of what to do next, Barney noticed Dizzy Rabbit and Spike Hedgehog making their way through the trees. Dizzy and Spike were often in trouble, so Barney hid behind a tree to watch them. They were both carrying bottles which made Barney think about the glass that had hurt Echo.

Dizzy and Spike sat down on an old log by the stream and started to drink bottles of beer and smoke cigarettes.

Barney watched in shock! Spike finished her drink first then threw the bottle into the grass where it broke into jagged pieces. The pair laughed loudly. They seemed to think it was clever and funny to break the bottles.

Watching Dizzy and Spike made Barney very angry. He wanted to come out from the trees and tell them about what had happened to Echo, but Barney wasn't sure what they might do if he told them to stop.

Instead, Barney decided to tell the Treetop Council so that they could clean up the mess and would later tell Dizzy and Spike how silly and selfish they had been. Barney lifted his wings and was just about to fly off when he heard a loud noise behind him. He stopped and looked around.

There was a lot of scraping and scratching followed by a big pile of earth rising up from the ground. Digsby Mole popped his head out of the top.

"Hi Barney," said Digsby excitedly.

"I got these sweets from some of the bigger kids down by the shops. Would you like some?"

Barney was surprised! "Er... no thank you," he said, backing away from Digsby.

"I don't know what they are. You know, Digsby, you should always tell your parents or a teacher if someone offers you something like that, you never know they could be pills not sweets."

Digsby laughed.

"They are only sweets. The bigger kids told me so. Here, take some."

"No," replied Barney firmly.

"Oh you are such a coward, Barney," said Digsby.

Colour the mirrors

Colour in the mirrors that describe how you think the woodland animals would feel (you can colour in more than one mirror).

When Dizzy smoked cigarettes, he felt:

Cool

Foolish

Big

When Spike drank alcohol, she felt:

Clever

Funny

Tough

When Barney saw Dizzy and Spike smoking and drinking he felt:

Worried

Unhappy

Afraid

Find the correct word from the vocabulary box, fill in the sentence and then complete the puzzle to reveal the hidden message.

1. D_____ can affect the way your body works.

2. T_____ drugs can damage your health and mind.

3. Drinking a_____ affects your behaviour.

4. Children and y_____ people should not drink alcohol.

5. S_____ can harm your health.

6. A_____ tell an adult you trust if someone offers you drugs or alcohol.

7. Drugs and alcohol are h_____, especially to young people.

8. Children must keep themselves h_____.

healthy	smoking	young	drugs
taking	alcohol	always	harmful

Barney didn't feel like a coward. He knew it was wrong to take pills or
sweets without knowing exactly what they were, but it still hurt being
called names so he decided it was time to leave.

Soon Barney was flying high over the tree tops. As he looked down,
he could see all of the broken glass, he spotted Dizzy, Spike and
Digsby standing by the old mill in the middle of the mess.

"Coward! Coward! Coward!" they all shouted.

Remember

If someone offers you drugs or alcohol:

Say no - be polite but firm.

Move away from them.

Tell an adult you can trust - a parent or teacher.

Never take anything from someone you don't trust.

If you find a needle, never pick it up, touch it or even kick it. Tell an adult straight away.

Keep yourself safe!

The following day, Barney went back to see Echo and told him
all about what had happened.

"What did they call you?" said Echo.

"A coward," replied Barney sadly.

"Well, I think that you were very sensible and not a coward at all," said
Echo, realising that being called a coward had hurt Barney's feelings.

Barney sighed. "Some people don't seem to care about anything.
It's very dangerous to take pills, smoke or drink alcohol. If only they
could see what might happen to them if they carry on this way."

Word Jumble

Un-scramble the letters to find the correct words.

GURDS

GAMIC RORIMR

TOCABOC

HOLCOAL

NARYEB

YSA ON

GIBDSY

KIPES

ZYIDZ

HOEC

MOT TAOTS

Wordsearch

See if you can find the following words:

1) Echo hurt his leg on sharp **GLASS**

2) Tom Stoat gave Barney a Magic **MIRROR**

3) Dizzy worried smoking cigarettes would affect his **RUNNING**

4) The Magic Mirror can see into the **FUTURE**

5) Digsby mistook **DRUGS** for sweets

6) Dizzy, Spike and Digsby later felt **ASHAMED**

7) The Mirror taught Dizzy, Spike and Digsby a **LESSON**

8) The Magic Mirror taught the friends to **CHANGE**

9) After stopping smoking & drinking the animals felt **HEALTHY**

10) Barney says make good **DECISIONS**

```
g a s h a m e d o d
l m i r r o r c u e
a e r u n n i n g c
s t s c h a n g e i
s o n s l v a y a s
r y i e o w k p n i
w l k o e n x r h o
h e a l t h y c d n
d r u g s p s t p s
f u t u r e l n o c
```

Then Barney had a brilliant idea, he put the mirror in the grass so Dizzy could easily find it.

That evening, Barney watched as Dizzy wandered through the trees and out into the clearing by the old mill as he had done every night that week. In his hand was a packet of cigarettes.

"I wonder where Digsby and Spike are tonight?" thought Dizzy while lighting a cigarette.

Then, as he was waiting, Dizzy noticed something shining in the grass. At first it just looked like more broken glass, but then he realised that it was actually a mirror.

Remember

Good decisions

It is not always easy to make the right decision. Other people may tell you or ask you to do something that you may not want to do. Here are some hints about how you can help yourself make good decisions.

Stop: Pause before you do or say anything.

Think: Ask yourself some questions. Is it the right thing to do? Will it harm me? Will it harm or hurt someone else? If I do it, will I keep myself safe? Can it affect the way I behave?

Consider: What is the right thing to do to keep yourself safe?

Decide: Make your choice.

Remember, make your own decisions and don't be influenced by someone if you know what they are doing is wrong.

Dizzy was curious and picked up the mirror wondering who could have left it there. He couldn't help but look into it. At first there was nothing special. It was just his own reflection staring back at him, but then Dizzy watched as it started to change.

He was no longer on his own by the old mill. Now there were lots of other people there too. They were watching him run a race and he was coming last. Dizzy couldn't understand it. He was the fastest rabbit in Treetop Forest. He had never been beaten in a race before, but there he was, puffing and panting and looking very miserable.

Dizzy had seen himself in the future. Smoking cigarettes is very bad for your health, especially when you are young like Dizzy. Suddenly smoking didn't seem so clever anymore.

Dizzy Rabbit

Activity

Can you design an anti-smoking poster, to help show Dizzy the error of his ways...

Dizzy didn't like looking at his reflection in the mirror and sat thinking about what it all meant. A few moments later, Spike arrived, with a bag full of bottles.

"What have you got in your hand?" she asked.

Dizzy didn't know what to say, so he just handed the mirror to Spike.

Just like Dizzy, Spike saw only herself at first. Then, as she was about to put the mirror down and reach for another bottle, she saw the image changing. There was a high fence around the clearing now with a big red sign that read DANGER KEEP OUT.

Inside the fence all she could see was lots of broken glass, rusted cans and other rubbish. It didn't look like a safe place to be. How did it get like that, she wondered?

The mirror changed again. This time Spike saw her mum reading the sign by the fence. She had a big white bandage on her leg.

Spike's mum had cut her leg on the broken glass and was very upset.

The mirror showed her how drinking alcohol had affected her behaviour. It was Spike and her friends that had caused the mess and because of their actions no-one could use the clearing anymore as it was no longer safe.

Suddenly drinking alcohol and throwing bottles around didn't seem so funny anymore.

Help get Spike through the maze to find her friends

START

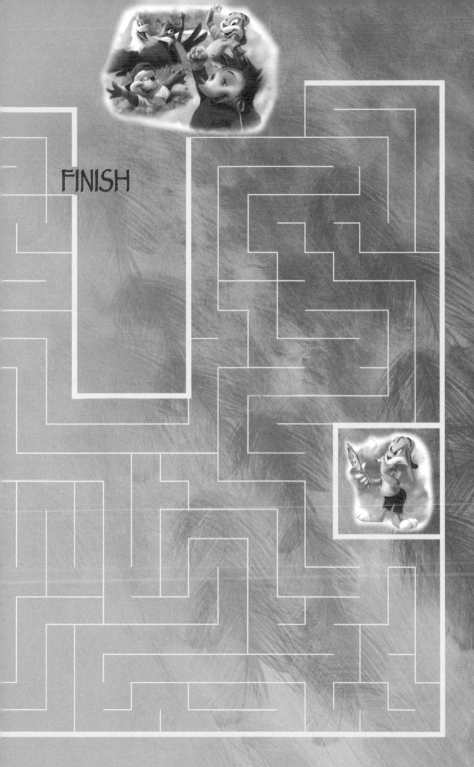

FINISH

Activity

Help Digsby Mole spot the 10 differences

As she was putting the mirror down, Spike noticed a message written on the back. She was about to read it when Digsby popped up right in front of her.

"Hi guys!" said Digsby with a big smile. "What's up?"

Dizzy and Spike were both feeling more than a little ashamed.

"We think you should take a look at this," said Dizzy quietly.

"OK, pass it here then," replied the mole.

What Digsby saw soon wiped the smile from his face.
He was being chased by a police officer.

The officer was about to take Digsby off to jail.

The sweets he had been given and tried to pass on to Barney
weren't sweets at all. They were drugs!

Activity

Draw a line to the part of the body which is put under strain by drugs, alcohol & tobacco

Draw a line to the part of the body which can cause you to become confused under the influence of alcohol or drugs

Smoking causes bad breath. Draw a line to the part of the body affected

Draw a line to the part of the body damaged most by alcohol

Draw a line to the part of the body that can make you sick when you drink alcohol

Draw a line to the part of the body damaged most by smoking

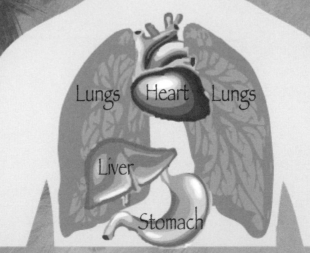

Brain

Mouth

Lungs   Heart   Lungs

Liver

Stomach

Wordsearch

See if you can find the following words:

1) Alcohol and Drugs can affect your **MOOD**
2) Cigarettes are **ADDICTIVE**
3) Alcohol, Drugs and Cigarettes **DAMAGE** your health
4) Cigarettes can make you **COUGH**
5) Alcohol can harm your **LIVER**
6) Alcohol can make you **SICK**
7) Drugs and Alcohol can put you in **DANGER**
8) Taking Drugs can seriously **HURT** you
9) Drugs can cause you to lose **CONTROL**
10) Drugs are **ILLEGAL**

m	a	d	d	i	c	t	i	v	e
o	d	d	r	d	u	i	y	n	o
o	f	t	s	a	y	l	c	c	b
d	a	m	a	g	e	l	o	o	a
i	o	o	m	u	a	e	u	n	d
q	s	e	b	e	x	g	g	t	a
l	i	v	e	r	h	a	h	r	n
q	c	w	z	x	u	l	q	o	g
y	k	b	q	y	r	m	l	l	e
i	n	x	x	n	t	z	c	f	r

Dizzy, Spike and Digsby were all shocked by what they had seen. It was nearly dark now and suddenly none of them felt very brave or tough. In fact, they all felt rather sorry for themselves; their futures didn't seem very bright at all.

What would you do?　　Activity

Who would you tell if someone offered you drugs or alcohol?

....

What would you say to someone if they offered you drugs or alcohol?

....

Can you list three reasons why you shouldn't take drugs or drink alcohol?

1..

2..

....

3..

....

What would you say to someone who asked you to smoke a cigarette?

....

....

....

If someone said, "I won't be your friend if you don't do what I want", what could you do?

....

....

....

Barney and Echo had been watching from a nearby tree. Echo's leg was feeling much better and he could run and jump as fast as ever.

Echo looked at Barney. "Do you think we should go and talk to them now?" he asked.

"Yes," replied Barney. "I think they have learned a big lesson, don't you?"

Barney and Echo went over to the log where the three animals sat looking very miserable.

"Why are you all looking so sad?" said Barney.

"Dizzy found this mirror and now we've all seen what is going to happen to us in the future," replied Spike, looking at her feet and scuffing her heels on the ground.

"Is that so?" said Echo, smiling.

"Yes, and it's not funny at all," said Dizzy. "I won't be able to run fast anymore, there will be a big fence to stop us playing here and poor Digsby will get sent to jail. Even Spike's mum will get hurt by all the broken glass we've left behind."

"If only we could stop it all happening," said Digsby.

"Well, maybe you can," replied Barney mysteriously.

Barney showed them the writing etched on the back of the mirror.

CHANGE
AND
THE
FUTURE
CHANGES
WITH YOU

"Change and the future changes with you," said all three animals together.

Dizzy, Spike and Digsby went home to think about what their futures might hold.

Barney Eagle

Barney needs to write a letter to Spike to explain why she should stop drinking alcohol, can you help Barney to write the letter below...

Two Weeks later...

Life in the forest quickly returned to normal once the Treetop Council had safely cleared up all the mess. All the animals could play without worrying about getting called names or injuring themselves on broken bottles and soon everyone was much happier.

Earlier in the day, Tom Stoat had told Barney and Echo that Dizzy and Spike wanted to meet them down by the old mill, so here they were, wondering and waiting.

Join the words to the matching statements using a line. The first one is done for you.

Alcohol   Can keep you safe.

Consequences   Are drugs which are taken to make
                           you better when you are ill.

Good decisions   Is a drug found in cigarettes.
                           Smoking can cause diseases
                           which harm our bodies.

Medicines   Is a drink which can affect the way
                           your brain and body works. The
                           effects can be harmful.

Nicotine   Are a result of your actions
                           (e.g. if you throw a stone
                           at a window it may break).

First to arrive was Dizzy who appeared from the trees with a massive hop, skip and then a big jump into the air.

"Hello Barney," shouted the rabbit before zooming off around the trees and almost crashing into the eagle as he ran back.

"Slow down a moment, Dizzy," said Barney. "Can't stop, I'm in training for the Forest Finals. I'm going to show everyone I'm the fastest rabbit in Treetop Forest," said Dizzy.

Barney laughed.

"Look, here comes Spike," said Echo. Then, remembering what the Hedgehog had seen in the mirror, he added: "How is your mum's foot, Spike? Did she cut it like I did on the broken glass?"

"No," replied Spike happily. "After looking in the mirror, I got such a fright that I stopped drinking alcohol and smashing bottles. Mum is great and, as you can see, there is no fence to keep us out of the clearing. I changed my ways and the future changed with me."

Barney was very pleased that Dizzy and Spike had changed their ways. But what about poor Digsby? Had he ended up in jail after all?

Then Barney heard a familiar scraping and scratching sound. He knew straight away what that meant.

"Digsby," he called, as the mole's head appeared from the ground. "Are you alright?"

"Never better, Barney," replied Digsby.

"I gave those pills I had to the police and I stopped going to the shops where the bigger kids hang out. I feel much, much better now. I changed..."

"We know," said Barney, Echo, Spike and Dizzy together. "You changed and the future changed with you."

Good Decisions

Dizzy has asked you to try a cigarette. You need to make a good decision. Colour in the explosions you would use to make a good decision.

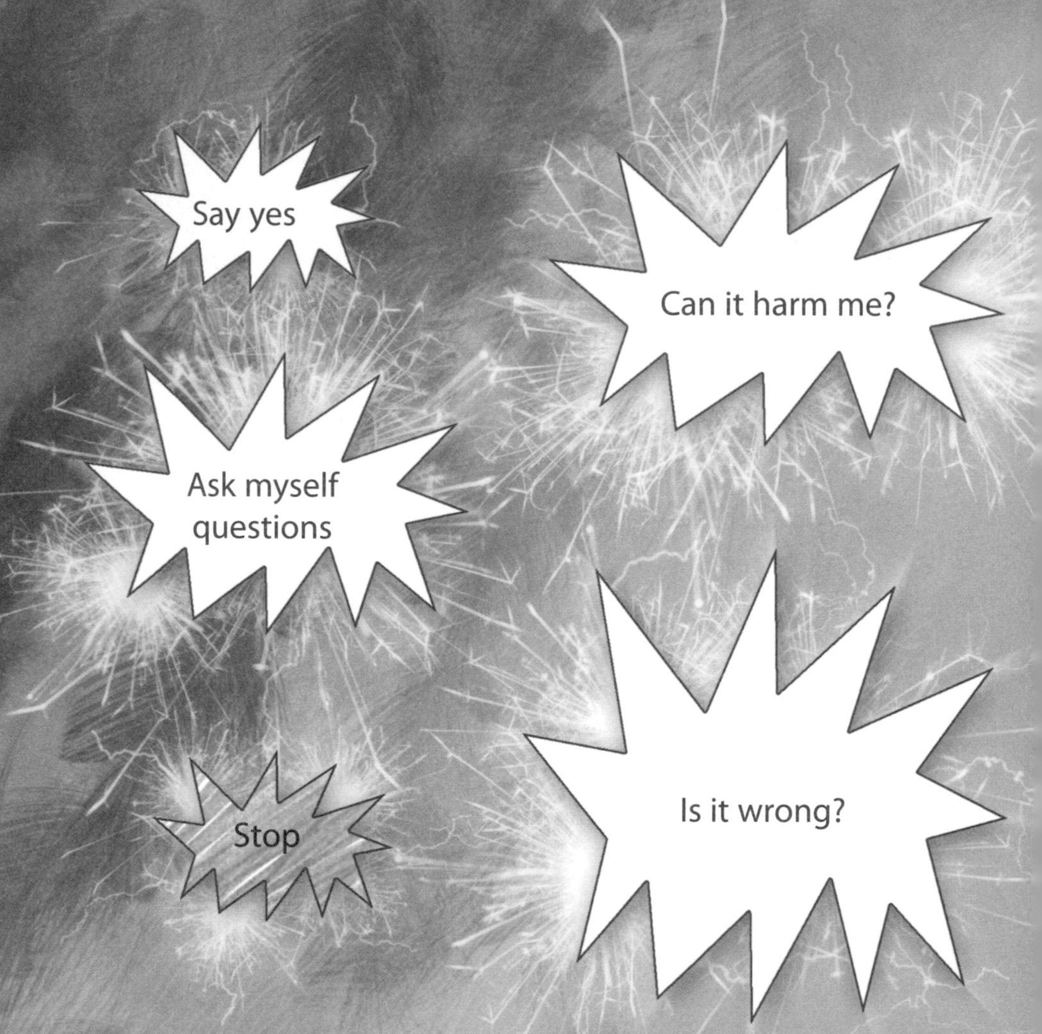

Say yes

Can it harm me?

Ask myself questions

Stop

Is it wrong?

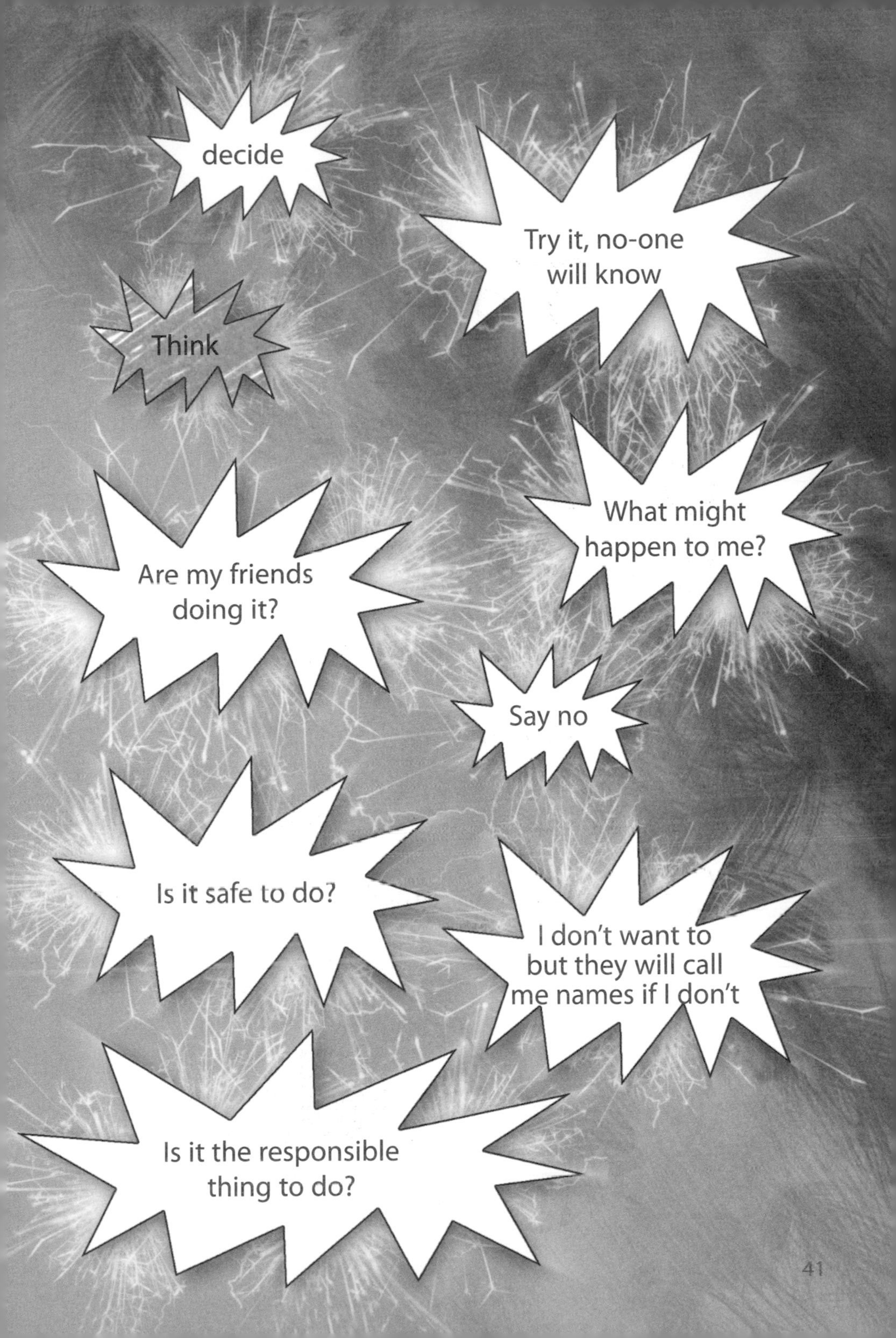

decide

Try it, no-one
will know

Think

What might
happen to me?

Are my friends
doing it?

Say no

Is it safe to do?

I don't want to
but they will call
me names if I don't

Is it the responsible
thing to do?

Tobacco

Talk to your parents & teachers

Only you can choose

Be smart, don't start

Addiction is hard to break

Consider your actions

Chemicals in cigarettes harm your body

Once you start smoking its hard to stop

True or false?
Tobacco

Activity

Parent activity

Answer the true or false questions below, then take this book home and get your parents or guardians involved by answering the questions too...

Circle the correct answer.

	Your Answer	Parents Answer
1. You can legally buy cigarettes at 14 years old.	True False	True False
2. Smoking causes bad breath, stained teeth, gum disease and your sense of taste.	True False	True False
3. Smoking is not addictive and its easy to stop.	True False	True False
4. If you smoke, your skin ages more quickly.	True False	True False
5. Your lungs can be very badly affected by smoking increasing the risk of serious disease.	True False	True False
6. Smoking will increase the risk of a heart attack.	True False	True False
7. Smoking can cause your bones to become weak and brittle.	True False	True False
8. Secondhand smoke is not harmful.	True False	True False
9. More than 80% of secondhand smoke is invisible and odourless.	True False	True False
10. Children are especially vulnerable to secondhand smoke.	True False	True False

Don't forget to bring the book back into school!

Alcohol

Alcohol harms your body

Listen to your parents & teachers

Choose with knowledge

Only you can say No

Health = Happiness

Obey the law

Leave Alcohol Alone

True or false? Alcohol

Parent activity

Answer the true or false questions below, then take this book home and get your parents or guardians involved by answering the questions too...

Circle the correct answer.

		Your Answer		Parents Answer	
1.	You can legally buy alcohol at 16 years old.	True	False	True	False
2.	Alcohol can make you feel sick.	True	False	True	False
3.	Drinking alcohol can change your mood and behaviour.	True	False	True	False
4.	It is just as safe for children to drink alcohol as it is for adults.	True	False	True	False
5.	Drinking alcohol helps you concentrate.	True	False	True	False
6.	Drinking alcohol can harm your brain, heart and liver.	True	False	True	False
7.	Drinking alcohol can lead to bad behaviour.	True	False	True	False
8.	Drinking alcohol will make you look cool.	True	False	True	False
9.	The older you are before starting to drink the less likley you are to have health problems.	True	False	True	False
10.	Drinking too much is always harmful and can be dangerous.	True	False	True	False

Don't forget to bring the book back into school!

True or false?
Drugs

Remember

Don't take any drugs

Resist peer pressure

Understand the consequences

Grow up healthy

Say no to drugs

Parent activity

Answer the true or false questions below, then take this book home and get your parents or guardians involved by answering the questions too...

Circle the correct answer.

	Your Answer	Parents Answer
1. Drugs are addictive.	True False	True False
2. Taking drugs will get you in trouble with the police.	True False	True False
3. Taking drugs can harm your relationship with friends and family.	True False	True False
4. Drugs can cause serious health problems.	True False	True False
5. Taking drugs can lead to bad behaviour.	True False	True False

Don't forget to bring the book back into school!

A message from Barney

You don't need a magic mirror to look into the future.

Drugs, alcohol and cigarettes harm your body.

Make good decisions and stay healthy.

Notes

··

··

··

··

··

··

··

··

··

··

··